Steck Vaughn

Maps Globes Graphs

Level A

Writer
Henry Billings

Consultants

Marian Gregory
Teacher
San Luis Coastal Unified School District
San Luis Obispo, California

Gloria Sesso
Supervisor of Social Studies
Half Hollow Hills School District
Dix Hills, New York

Norman McRae, Ph.D.
Former Director of Fine Arts and Social Studies
Detroit Public Schools
Detroit, Michigan

Edna Whitfield
Former Social Studies Supervisor
St. Louis Public Schools
St. Louis, Missouri

Marilyn Nebenzahl
Social Studies Consultant
San Francisco, California

Karen Wiggins
Director of Social Studies
Richardson Independent School District
Richardson, Texas

Check the Maps•Globes•Graphs Website to find more fun geography activities at home.

Go to www.HarcourtAchieve.com/mggwelcome.html

Harcourt Achieve
Rigby • Steck-Vaughn

www.HarcourtAchieve.com
1.800.531.5015

Acknowledgments

Cartography

Land Registration and Information Service
    Amherst, Nova Scotia, Canada
Gary J. Robinson
MapQuest.com, Inc.
R.R. Donnelley and Sons Company
XNR Productions Inc., Madison, Wisconsin

Photography Credits
COVER (globe, clouds), pp. 4, 5 (both), 6 (both), 8 © PhotoDisc; pp. 12, 13 David McKenzie; pp. 16, 17 Stan Kearl; p. 21 © Graphic Eye/Tony Stone Images; p. 22 David Phillips; p. 24 David Phillips; p. 25 Gary Russ; p. 27 © Mark Segal/TSW-Click/Chicago; p. 30 David McKenzie; p. 36 David McKenzie; p. 44 (t) © Larry Lefever/Grant Heilman Photography; p. 44 (b) Stan Kearl; p. 52 © Index Stock International, Inc.; p. 52 (inset) David McKenzie; p. 63 © PhotoDisc

Illustration Credits
David Griffin pp. 9, 10, 14, 15, 21, 23, 25, 28, 29, 42, 50; Michael Krone pp. 18, 19, 20, 37, 38, 41; T.K. Riddle pp. 31, 32, 33, 34, 35, 44, 45, 46, 47, 48; Rusty Kaim p. 4

ISBN 0-7398-9101-4

© 2004 Harcourt Achieve Inc.

12 13 14 15 16 17 18   1678   15 14 13 12 11

4500318556

Contents

Geography Themes

Geography is the study of Earth and its people. We can tell about geography in five ways.

- **Location**
- **Place**
- **Human/Environment Interaction**
- **Movement**
- **Regions**

Location tells where something is. It tells what something is near.

Kami lives in an apartment.
It is in a big city.
It is near a park.

1. What is near your home?

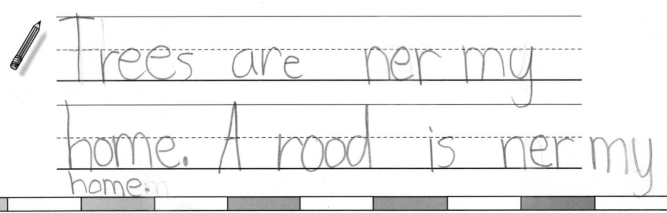

Trees are ner my home. A rood is ner my home.

Place tells what a location is like.

Lara lives in a crowded city.
The buildings are very close together.
There are no trees or grassy yards.

2. What is it like where you live?

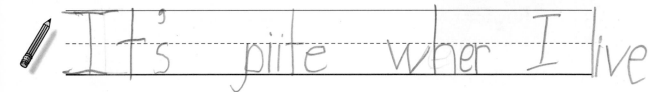

It's piite wher I live

Human/Environment Interaction tells how people
live in a place.

Casey lives on a horse farm.
His family uses the land to raise
horses.
Casey likes to help with the
horses.

3. How do people use the land where you live?

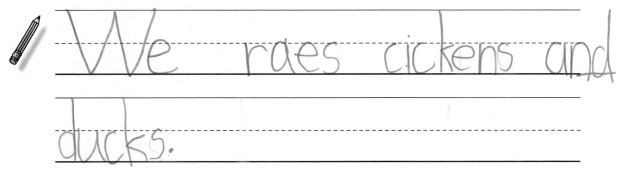

We raes cickens and
ducks.

Movement tells how people get from place to place.

Hana and Miki walk to school.
Some days they ride their bicycles.

4. How do you get to school?

I ride the bus.

Regions tell how parts of Earth are alike.

Katrina lives in a mountain
  region.
The winters are very cold.
The mountains are covered
  with snow.

5. Do you live on flat land, a hill, or a mountain?

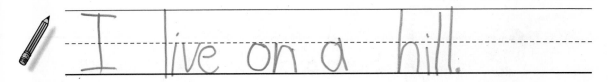
I live on a hill.

Draw a picture of the place where you live.

6. Circle the name of your favorite time of the year.

Fall   (Winter)   Spring   Summer

7. What is your favorite season like?

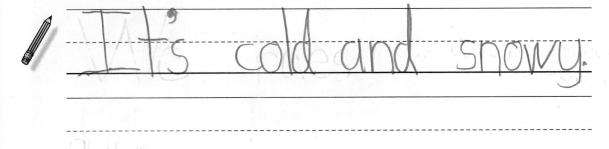
It's cold and snowy.

This is a **photo**.

It is a picture made by a .

Name _____

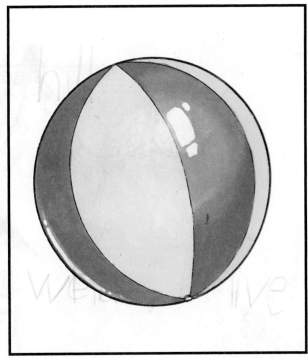
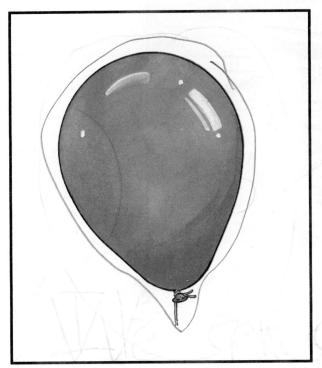

These are **drawings**.
Which drawings are of things in the photo?
Circle them.

Finding Things in a Picture

This is a drawing of the photo.
It shows the same place.

1. Color the balloons.

2. Color the hat.

3. Color the cake.

Finding Things in a Picture

This drawing shows a house.

1. Color the doors brown.
2. Color the trees green.
3. Color the steps yellow.

Match a Photo and a Drawing

Color the rest of the drawing.
Match the colors you see in the photo.

Name _____

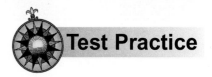

Skill Check

Words I Know   **photo**   **drawing**

Write each word under a picture.

photo   _drawing_

Reading a Picture

1. Color the house yellow.

2. Color the bicycle red.

3. Color the car blue.

Movement tells how people and goods get from one place to another. People and goods can move in an airplane, a train, a truck, or a ship.

1. Draw a line and match each word with its picture.

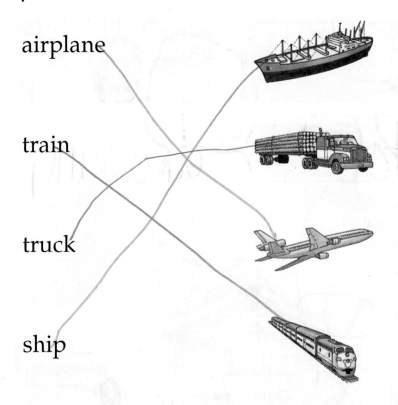

airplane

train

truck

ship

2. What is another way people and goods move?

car

Sometimes movement means how ideas are spread. We get ideas from a newspaper. We get ideas from television.

3. Look at the drawing.
   Circle the ways to get ideas.

This photo shows a park.
It was taken from the ground.
What things do you see?

This photo shows the same park.
It was taken from above.
What else do you see?

Finding Things in a Picture

This drawing shows the same park.

1. Color the trees and grass green.

2. Color the pool blue.

3. Color the swing yellow.

4. Color the fence brown.

Name _____

Finding Things in a Picture

What does this drawing show?

1. Color the bed blue.

2. Color the table yellow.

3. Color the books green.

4. Color the toys red.

Finding Things in a Picture

What does this drawing show?

1. Color the bus yellow.

2. Color one car red.

3. Color two cars blue.

4. Color the truck orange.

Name _____

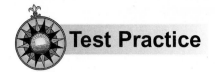

Skill Check

Color the kites in the sky.
Match the colors you see in the photo.

This photo shows a neighborhood.
What do you see in the photo?

Name _____

Here is the same neighborhood.
This is a **map.**

1. Two houses are not colored. Color them yellow.

2. Find the streets. Color them gray.

Making a Map From a Photo

1. Draw the pool on the map. Color it blue.

2. Color the rest of the map.
   Match the colors you see in the photo.

Name _____

Making a Map From a Photo

1. Some cars are missing on the map.
   Add them to the map.

2. Color the rest of the map.
   Match the colors you see in the photo.

Finding Things on a Map

This map shows a pet store.

1. Color the fish orange.

2. Color the dog brown.

3. Add a turtle to the map.

4. Color the turtles green.

Name _____

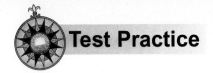

Skill Check

Words I Know   **map**

Write the word <u>map</u> under the map.
Write the word <u>photo</u> under the photo.

photo   *map*

1. Look at the map. Color the building brown.

2. Add the boat to the map.

3. Add the bridge to the map.

4. Color the water blue.

Geography Themes Up Close

Place tells what it is like somewhere. Some places have many trees. Some places have many buildings.

1. Draw a line and match each place name with its picture.

city

park

farm

store

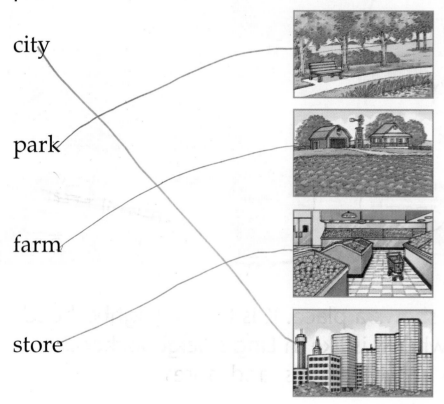

2. What is another kind of place?

beach

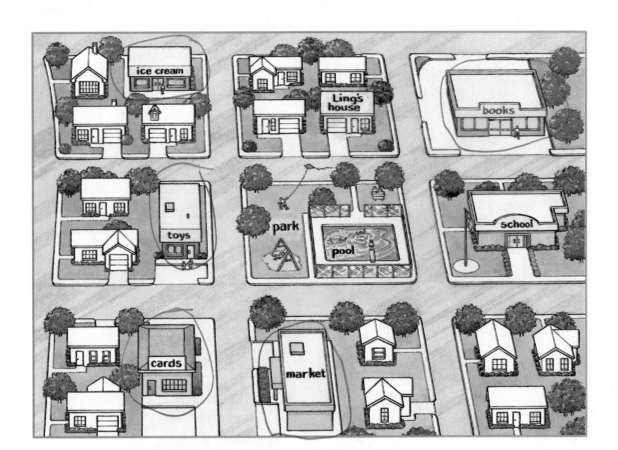

This map shows a place. It is Ling's neighborhood.
It shows what it is like in Ling's neighborhood.
There are houses, streets, and stores.

3. Color Ling's house yellow.

4. Circle the stores.

5. Name one other thing in Ling's neighborhood.

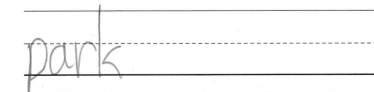

park

Four Sides

This photo has four sides.

The chalkboard is at the **top**.

The desks are at the **bottom**.

The flag is at the **right**.

The globe is at the **left**.

Name _____

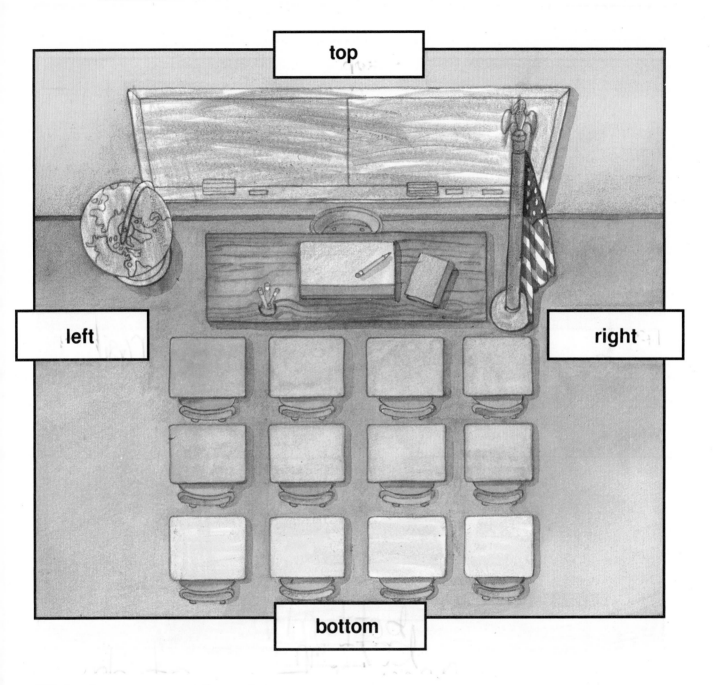

top

left

right

bottom

This is a map of a classroom.

1. Color the chalkboard at the top green.

2. Color the desks at the bottom yellow.

3. Color the flagpole at the right red.

4. Color the globe at the left blue.

Finding Four Sides

1. Write <u>top</u>, <u>bottom</u>, <u>right</u> and <u>left</u> in the boxes.
2. Color the plane at the top red.
3. Color the sidewalk at the bottom brown.
4. Color the bus on the right yellow.
5. Color the car on the left green.

Finding Four Sides

1. Write <u>top</u>, <u>bottom</u>, <u>right</u> and <u>left</u> in the boxes.
2. Color two lions near the top yellow.
3. Color three monkeys near the bottom brown.
4. Color one elephant near the right gray.
5. Color four parrots near the left green.

Moving Toward Top, Bottom, Right, or Left

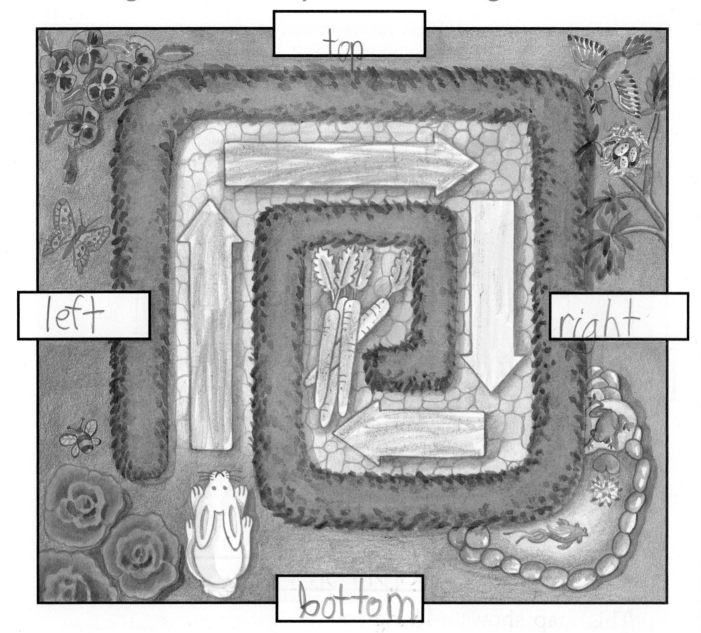

1. Write <u>top</u>, <u>bottom</u>, <u>right</u> and <u>left</u> in the boxes.
2. One arrow points to the top. Color it red.
3. One arrow points to the right. Color it green.
4. One arrow points to the bottom. Color it yellow.
5. One arrow points to the left. Color it blue.
6. Color the carrots.

Name _____

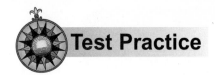
Skill Check

Words I Know   top   bottom   right   left

top

left

right

bottom

This map shows a living room.

1. Write <u>top</u>, <u>bottom</u>, <u>right</u> and <u>left</u> in the boxes.
2. Draw a sofa near the top.
3. Draw a TV near the bottom.
4. Color the chair near the right green.
5. Color the chair near the left brown.

North, south, east, and west are **directions**.
N, S, E, and W stand for north, south, east, and west.

The girl faces **north**. Find N in the photo.
South is behind her. Find S in the photo.
East is to her right. Find E in the photo.
West is to her left. Find W in the photo.

Name _____

This map shows a farm.
The top of the map is north.

Where is each thing?
Write <u>north</u>, <u>south</u>, <u>east</u>, and <u>west</u>.

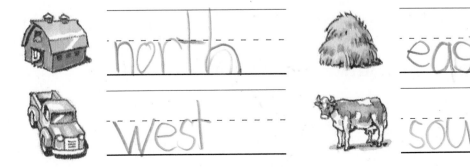

north   *east*

west   *south*

Finding Directions at the Fruit Market

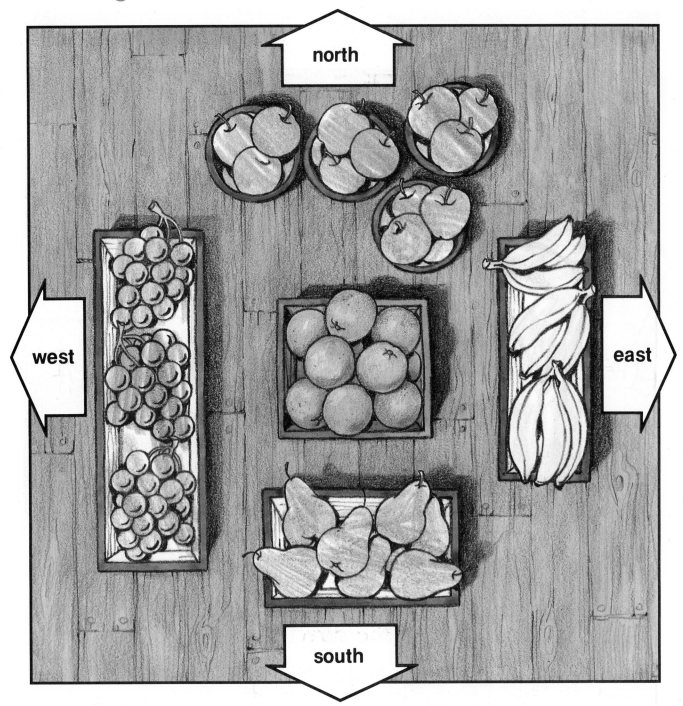

1. Which fruit is on the north side? Color it red.
2. Which fruit is on the south side? Color it green.
3. Which fruit is on the east side? Color it yellow.
4. Which fruit is on the west side? Color it purple.

Name _____

Finding Directions at the Park

Start at the flower gardens.
Draw an arrow to show where you go.
Then circle the letter of the direction you go.

1. Go to feed the . You go (N) E .

2. Next go to the . You go S (W) .

3. Then go to the . You go (S) N .

4. Now run to the . You run W (E) .

Finding Directions at the Fair

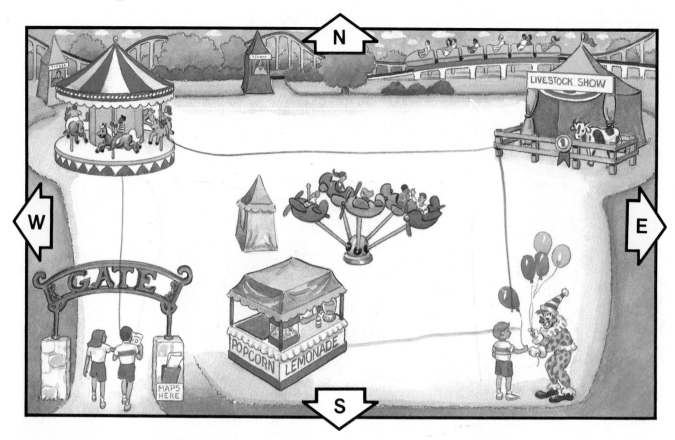

Get a map at the gate and have fun at the fair.
Draw an arrow to show where you go.
Write the direction you go to get

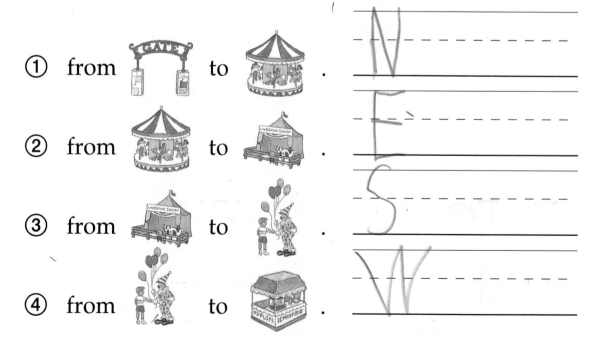

① from [GATE] to [carousel] . N

② from [carousel] to [LIVESTOCK SHOW] . E

③ from [LIVESTOCK SHOW] to [clown] . S

④ from [clown] to [POPCORN LEMONADE] . W

Name _____

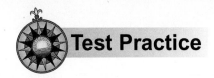

Skill Check

Words I Know **north   south   east   west**

Finding Directions on a Map

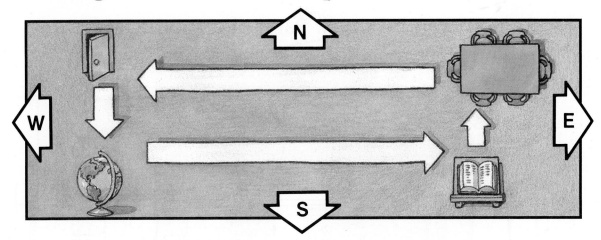

This map shows a library.

Write the direction that tells the way to get

① from to . <u>south</u>

② from to . <u>east</u>

③ from to . <u>north</u>

④ from to . <u>west</u>

Geography Themes Up Close

Regions are areas that are alike. Regions can be large like mountain regions.

Regions can be small. Parts of a room can be a region. This map shows a classroom.

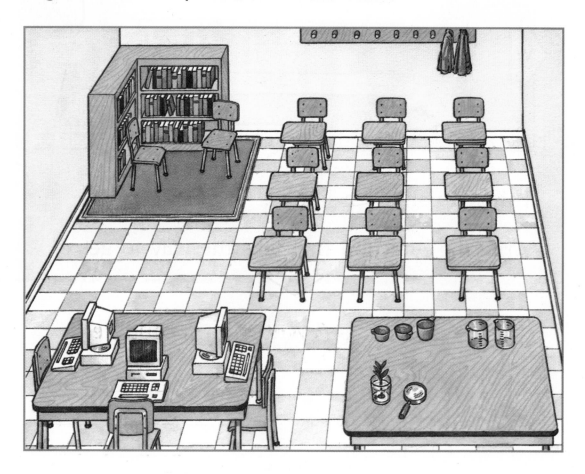

1. Put a ✔ on the science region.

2. Draw a circle around the computer region.

3. Draw an X on the reading region.

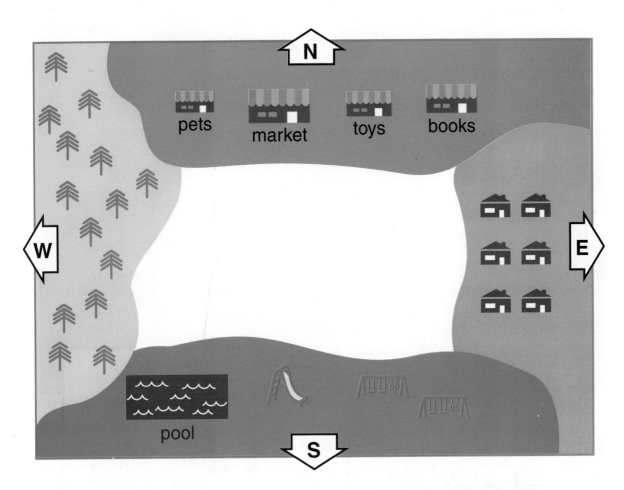

4. Where is each region? Write <u>north</u>, <u>south</u>, <u>east</u>, or <u>west</u>.

park _____   forest _____

houses _____   stores _____

The photo shows a real barn.
The drawing is a **symbol** for a barn.
A symbol stands for something real.

Match each symbol with a photo.

Name _____

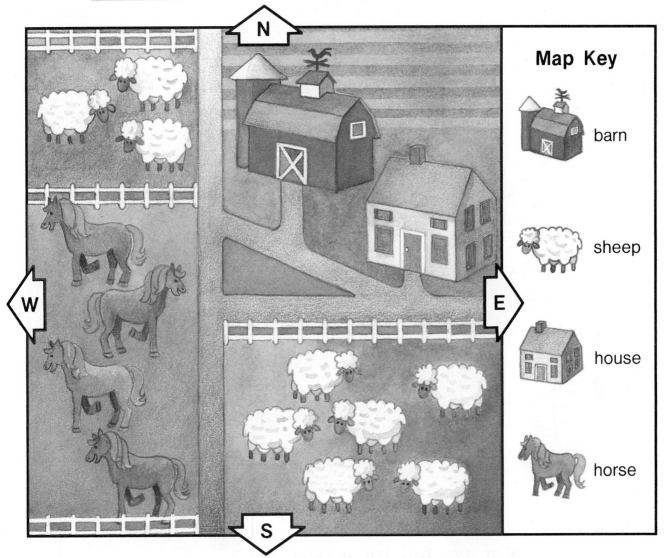

Map Key

barn

sheep

house

horse

This map shows a farm.
The **map key** tells what each symbol stands for.

Write what the symbols stand for.
The first one is done for you.

house

Finding Symbols on a Map

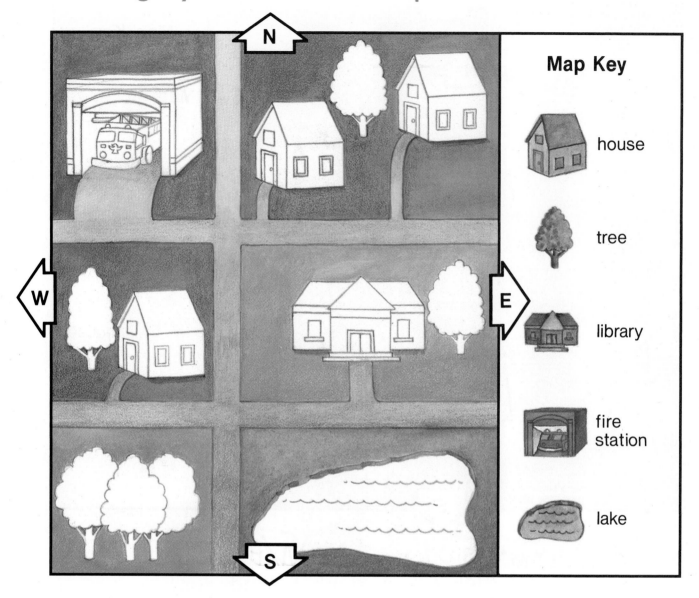

1. Find <u>N</u>, <u>S</u>, <u>E</u>, and <u>W</u> on the map.
2. Study the map key.
3. Find the trees on the map. Color them green.
4. Find the houses. Color them yellow.
5. Find the library. Color it brown.
6. Find the fire station. Color it red.
7. Find the lake. Color it blue.

Name _____

Finding Symbols on a Map

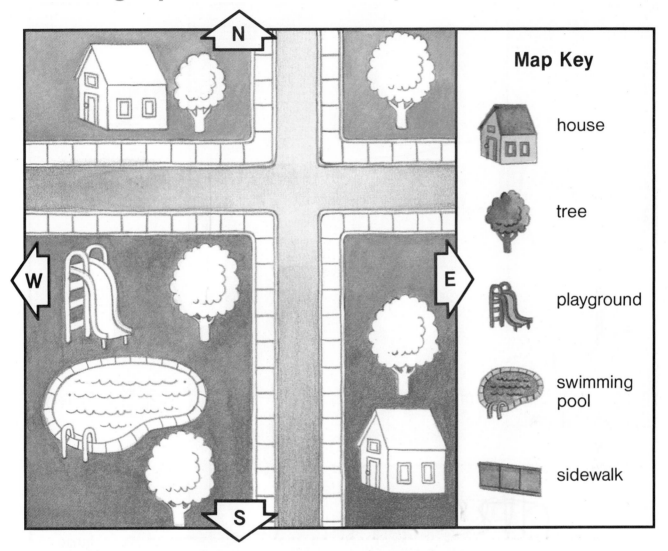

1. Find <u>N</u>, <u>S</u>, <u>E</u>, and <u>W</u> on the map.

2. Study the map key.

3. Find the houses on the map. Color them yellow.

4. Find the trees. Color them green.

5. Find the playground. Color it red.

6. Find the swimming pool. Color it blue.

7. Find the sidewalks. Color them brown.

Finding Symbols on a Map

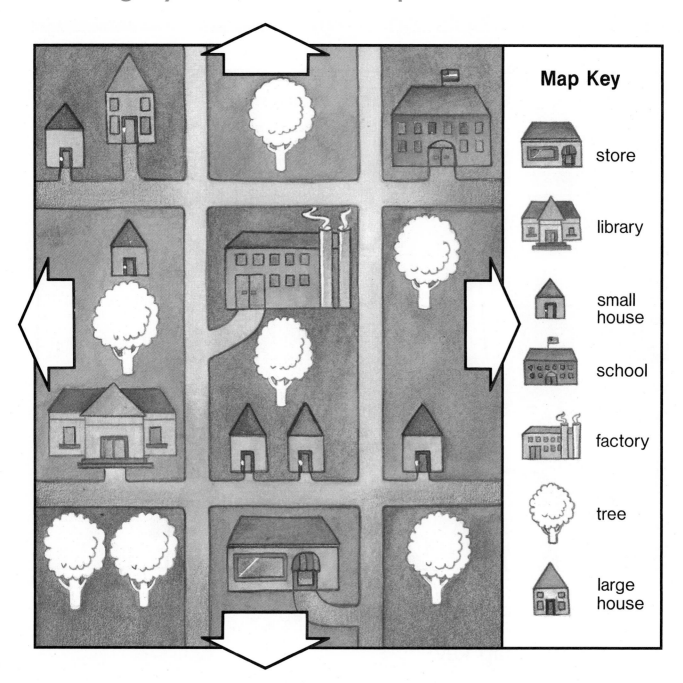

Map Key

store

library

small house

school

factory

tree

large house

1. Write <u>N</u>, <u>S</u>, <u>E</u>, and <u>W</u> where they belong.
2. Find the factory. Go south. Color that tree red.
3. Find the library. Go north. Color that tree blue.
4. Find the store. Go east. Color that tree green.
5. Find the school. Go west. Color that tree yellow.

Name _____

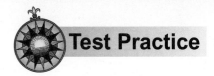

Skill Check

Words I Know   **symbol**   **map key**

_____

- - - - - - - - - - - - - - - - - - -

The _____ tells what each symbol stands for.

Reading a Map

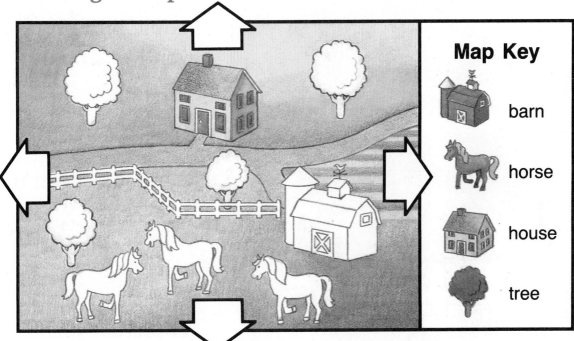

This map shows a farm.

1. Write <u>N</u>, <u>S</u>, <u>E</u>, and <u>W</u> where they belong.
2. Find the horses. Color them brown.
3. Find the barn. Color it red.
4. Find the house. Go west. Color that tree green.

Geography Themes Up Close

Human/Environment Interaction tells how people use the land where they live. They use rivers for water. They grow food on the land.

1. Match each picture with a sentence.

People build houses on the land.

People have fun in parks.

People use grass to feed animals.

People fish in lakes.

Sometimes people change the land. They build roads and bridges. They build houses or farms on the land.

2. Draw pictures that show how people change the land.

People build tall buildings.   People farm the land.

3. How have people changed the land where you live?

_____

- -

_____

- -

_____

The large photo shows **Earth**.
Earth is round like a ball.

The small photo shows a **globe**.
A globe is also round like a ball.
A globe is a **model** of Earth.

Name _____

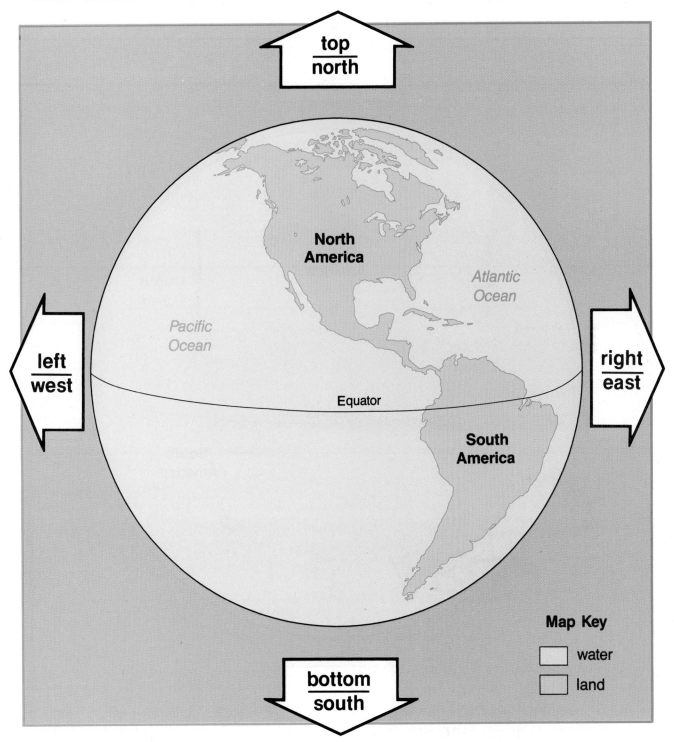

Look at the globe above.
The blue color stands for water.
The green color stands for land.
The words are names of real places.

Finding Places on a Globe

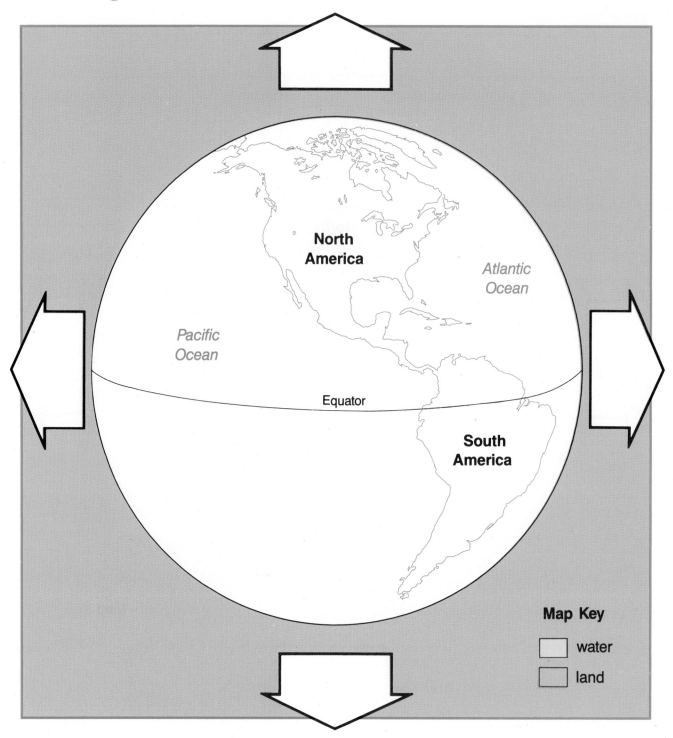

1. Write <u>north</u>, <u>south</u>, <u>east</u>, and <u>west</u> in the arrows.

2. Color the water blue.

3. Color the land green.

Name _____

Finding Places on a Globe

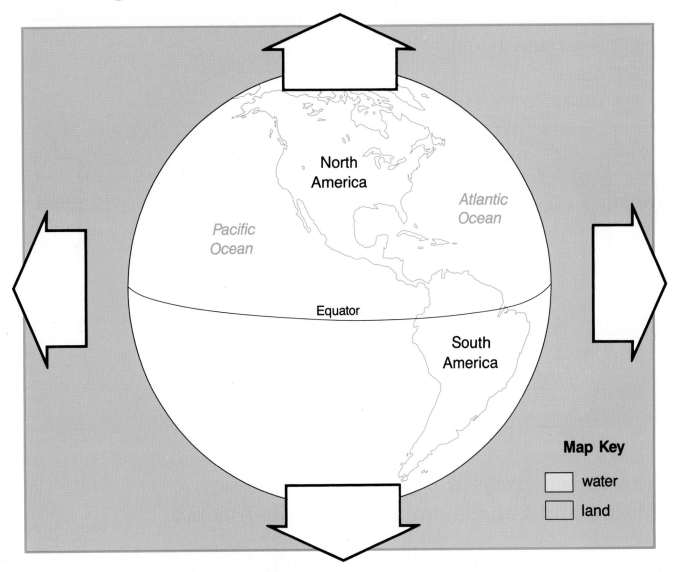

1. Write <u>N</u>, <u>S</u>, <u>E</u>, and <u>W</u> in the arrows.

2. Color the globe to match the map key.

3. Look at the land on the map.

4. Find the water to the east of the land.

_____

- - - - - - - - - - - - - - - - -

5. It is called the Atlantic _____.

Finding Places on a Globe

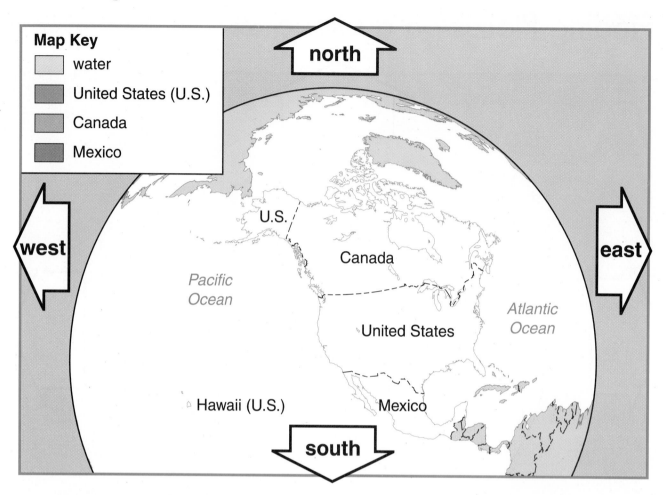

Map Key
- water
- United States (U.S.)
- Canada
- Mexico

north

west

east

U.S.

Canada

Pacific Ocean

Atlantic Ocean

United States

Hawaii (U.S.)

Mexico

south

The United States is part of North America.
Mexico and Canada are also in North America.

1. What country is south of the United States?

2. What country is north of the United States?

3. Color the map to match the map key.

Name _____

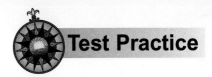

Skill Check

Words I Know   **globe**   **model**

_____

- - - - - - - - - - - - - -

A _____ looks like Earth.

Reading a Globe

Canada

United States

Atlantic Ocean

Mexico

Pacific Ocean

Map Key

☐ water

☐ United States (U.S.)

☐ Canada

☐ Mexico

_____

- - - - - - - - - - - - - -

1. The Atlantic Ocean is _____ of the United States.

_____

- - - - - - - - -

2. Canada is _____ of the United States.

_____

- - - - - - - - -

3. Mexico is _____ of the United States.

Geography Themes Up Close

Location tells where places are found. Every place on Earth has a location. Iowa is in the United States. It is west of Illinois.

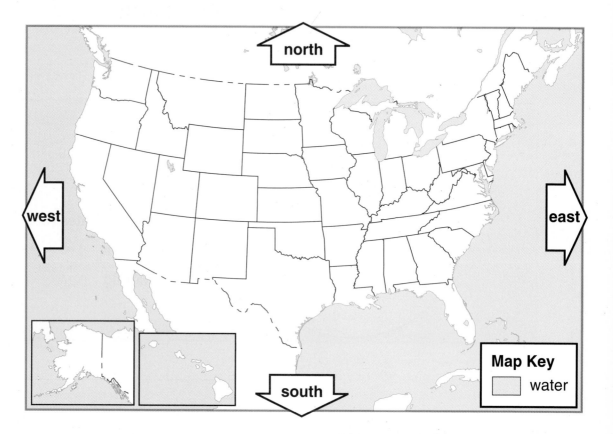

1. There are high mountains in the west.
   Put a red ✔ in the west.

2. There are many rivers in the east.
   Put a blue ✔ in the east.

3. There are some big lakes in the north.
   Circle the lakes in green.

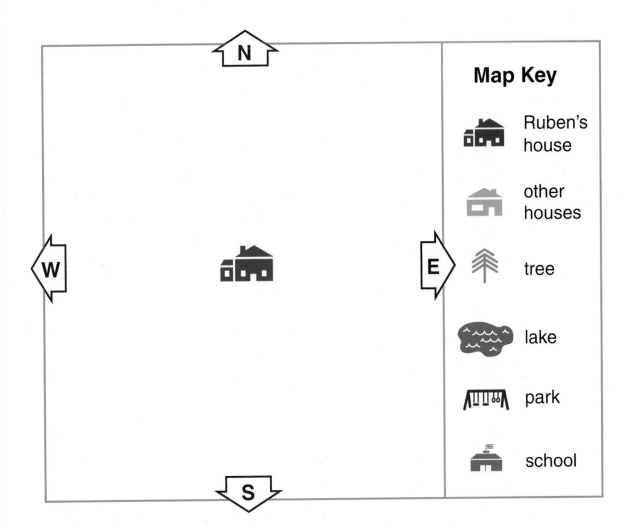

Look at the map of Ruben's neighborhood. Find Ruben's house. Circle it. Draw the rest of the map.

4. Draw a house east of Ruben's house.

5. Draw a lake north of Ruben's house.

6. Draw a park south of Ruben's house.

7. Draw a school west of Ruben's house.

Washington

Oregon

Idaho

Montana

North
Dakota

South
Dakota

Wyoming

Nebraska

west

Nevada

Utah

Colorado

Kansas

California

Arizona

New Mexico

Ok

Texas

Alaska

Hawaii

north

The United States

New Hampshire

Maine

Vermont

Massachusetts

Minnesota

Michigan

New York

Rhode Island

Wisconsin

Connecticut

Pennsylvania

New Jersey

Iowa

Ohio

Delaware

Indiana

Washington, D.C.

Illinois

West Virginia

Maryland

east

Virginia

Missouri

Kentucky

North Carolina

Tennessee

Arkansas

South Carolina

Alabama

Georgia

Mississippi

Louisiana

Florida

south

The World

north

south

east

west

Arctic Ocean

Pacific Ocean

Atlantic Ocean

Indian Ocean

Pacific Ocean

Asia

Europe

Africa

Australia

Antarctica

North America

South America

Glossary

bottom
page 30

Canada
page 56

directions
page 36

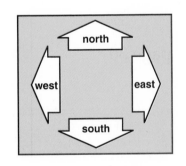

drawing
page 9

Earth
page 52

east
page 36

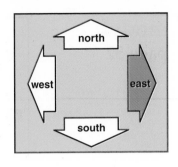

globe
page 52

left
page 30

map
page 23

map key
page 45

Mexico
page 56

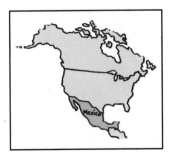

model
page 52

south
page 36

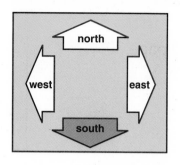

north
page 36

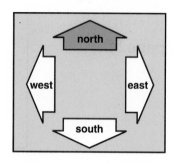

symbol
page 44

barn

ocean
page 55

top
page 30

photo
page 8

United States
page 56

right
page 30

west
page 36

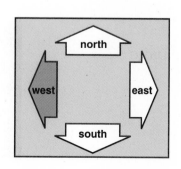